Compost

Compost

Ken Thompson

LONDON, NEW YORK, MUNICH,
MELBOURNE, DELHI

Project Editor Annelise Evans
Project Art Editor Clare Shedden

Senior Editor Helen Fewster
DTP Design Louise Waller
Pearson Picture Library Lucy Claxton
Picture Research Mel Watson
Jacket Concept Peter Luff
Production Liz Cherry
Managing Editor Anna Kruger
Managing Art Editor Alison Donovan
Indexer Michèle Clarke

Photographer Peter Anderson
Illustrator Mark Hudson

First published in Great Britain in 2007 by
Dorling Kindersley Limited,
80 Strand, London WC2R 0RL

Penguin Group

Copyright © 2007
Dorling Kindersley Limited
Text copyright © 2007 Ken Thompson

A CIP catalogue record is available
from the British Library

ISBN: 978 1 40531 103 8

Colour reproduction by MDP, UK
Printed and bound by Hung Hing, China

Discover more at
www.dk.com

Foreword

Few things are better for your plants and for the environment
than home-made garden compost, yet why is making it never
quite as straightforward as the experts would have us believe?
Perhaps unrealistic expectations, coupled with the modern desire
for instant results, are mainly to blame. The commercial garden
industry, keen to sell us a fancy machine or secret ingredient that
promises to make compost in days, merely adds to our feeling of
inadequacy. But don't panic, this book is here to help take the
mystery and fuss out of making compost.

It makes clear that compost making doesn't need to be
hard work, need cost almost nothing, and that the only secret
ingredient you need is patience. It doesn't prescribe any particular
approach, but it does explain that although things will go wrong,
if you understand the basic principles and learn from your
mistakes, you will soon arrive at a method that works for you
and suits your kind of gardening.

Before we start, just a comment about the word compost.
I'm using the word in the sense that most gardeners would
understand it, but of course there's another kind of compost,
in the sense of the stuff you fill pots with: potting compost. This
book isn't about that kind of compost, although garden compost
can be one ingredient of home-made potting compost.

Ken Thompson

Contents

Understanding compost: the right stuff

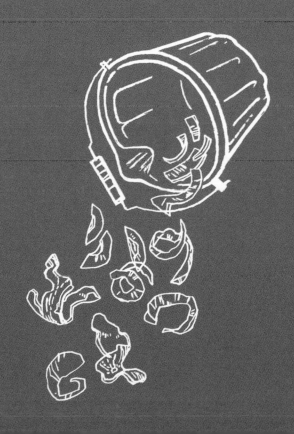

What is compost?

When animals and plants die, they decompose surprisingly quickly. The body of an adult human is reduced to a mere skeleton in about three weeks, if not artificially preserved. The bones last longer, but not a great deal. Shakespeare was right when his gravedigger in Hamlet (*Act V, Scene I*) estimated there was not much left of a cadaver after eight or nine years. Even huge trees go the same way, and about as quickly.

The end product of this composting process is a remarkably resistant and complex organic substance called humus, which is largely responsible for the brown colour of the majority of soils in temperate regions.

Humus is a mixture of the highly altered remains of the original organic matter – whether from plants or animals – that arrives at the soil surface, as well as new compounds made by bacteria and fungi. But only a small fraction of the original material is destined to become humus. Most simply disappears, returned to the carbon dioxide (CO_2), water, and mineral salts from which it was first made.

Somewhere in this process – between the large amount of original material and the tiny fraction that is left as humus – lies

what every gardener wants:
compost.

The entire composting process can be seen on any woodland floor. On the surface are freshly fallen, unaltered leaves. Dig down a little way and the leaves become more fragmented and much less distinct. Eventually, you will come to a dark, crumbly material in

which the original leaves are quite unrecognizable. This is usually called leafmould, but it's just a special variety of compost, made only from tree leaves rather than the usual mixture of materials.

In fact, the woodland floor tells us two important things about compost.

First, the transition from fresh material to finished compost is a gradual one, with the end point being entirely a matter of opinion. Second, if you were to rummage around in the leafmould, you would soon turn up a few clearly identifiable twigs. Larger pieces of tougher material (and twigs are both larger and tougher) decompose more slowly than smaller, softer material.

Compost is "finished" when the easily decomposed parts of the original material have disappeared, and the more resistant material has decomposed to the extent that it is no longer recognizable, yet the majority of the original organic matter and nutrients still remain.

Nevertheless, deciding when this perfect state has been achieved remains a personal matter, largely affected by how much twiggy stuff you are prepared to tolerate in the finished product. I can't tell you how to decide when your compost is finished, but I can tell you how to get there in a reasonable time.

Why compost?

There are plenty of very good reasons for gardeners to make compost but, above all, it spares the environment the damage caused by burying or burning waste, reduces the need to destroy natural habitats by excavating peat, and saves you money.

DON'T BIN IT, RECYCLE IT

UK households produced about 30 million tons of waste in 2002 — that's over 500kg (1,100lb) for every person in the country. This figure grows by about three per cent every year. Currently, only about ten per cent of British household waste is recycled, which puts the UK near the bottom of the European league. Some countries, like Germany and Denmark, do much better, although a few are even worse. Most waste is incinerated or ends up in landfill, yet about half of all household waste could be composted.

At the same time, every year gardeners across the world buy millions of tons of growing media, soil conditioners, and mulching materials, much of it based on peat. A high proportion of this could be replaced, free of charge, if gardeners recycled what they simply throw away.

Incinerated waste is returned immediately to the air as carbon dioxide (CO_2) and other gases, causing air pollution and contributing to global warming. Organic matter in landfill also slowly decays, but the main product is methane, an even worse greenhouse gas than CO_2, and 20 per cent of the UK's methane emissions come from biodegradable waste in landfill sites.

The soil is also the safest place for waste organic matter. Once returned to temperate soils as compost, some organic matter stays there, often for a long time. More widespread use of compost by farmers and gardeners could make a small but significant contribution to the commitments made in the Kyoto Protocol of 1997 to reduce CO_2 emissions.

TREAT YOUR SOIL

It's hard to believe just how many benefits compost provides for soil. Even when spread on the surface as a mulch, and long before it actually enters the soil, compost helps to suppress weeds, retains soil moisture in dry conditions, and protects soil from the damaging effects of wind and heavy rain.

But it's when organic matter gets into the soil that it really starts to work its magic. Soil structure depends almost entirely on organic matter. In a healthy soil, the organic humus and inert mineral particles are stuck together in tiny crumbs a millimetre or two across. These crumbs are held together by fine fungal strands, or hyphae, and by organic glues produced by trillions of bacteria.

One gram of healthy soil may contain up to 3km of fungal strands,

that's 54 miles of hyphae for every ounce of soil. And what do the fungi and bacteria eat? Organic matter.

The crumb structure of a healthy soil is an important factor in maintaining the soil's water supply, because tiny pores between the crumbs form a kind of "sponge" that is normally full of water. The soil is also full of larger channels, which fill with water after rain but are normally full of air. This air supply is vital, since plant roots and soil animals need to breathe. Most of these channels are created by earthworms, which eat – you guessed it – organic matter. The more compost you make and use on the soil, the better will be its crumb and pore structure, and the less need there will be to water your plants in dry weather.

Compost is also a valuable source of mineral nutrients, such as nitrogen (N) and phosphorus (P), that plants need for growth. As organic matter breaks down, the minerals are slowly released and made available to plants. This breakdown happens faster in warmer weather, which of course is when the plants need them most. Some kinds of organic matter break down and release their nutrients relatively quickly, while others go on to form humus, which provides a much longer-lived bank of nutrients in the soil.

Mycorrhizas, specialist symbiotic fungi that live on and in plant roots, also break down organic matter and transfer the nutrients directly to plants, helping to stop them being washed out of the soil and lost.

In short, plants need three key things from soil – water, air, and nutrients – and compost helps to provide all three.

GOOD LIFE FOR WILDLIFE

Soil is not inert: it is an almost unbelievably diverse, living community of microbes and animals. A single square metre (sq yd) of woodland floor is typically home to 30 million nematodes (eelworms) and 250 different species of mites. Unlike plants, the micro-organisms and animals of the soil community cannot make their own food and depend entirely on organic matter from the world above, so more organic matter means more microbes and more soil animals.

To a very large extent, everything else in the garden depends on the health of this soil community. A healthy soil means healthy plants, which provide plenty of nectar for pollinators and lots of leaves for the herbivorous insects that are eaten by beetles, birds, predatory wasps, and spiders.

The soil community also contributes directly to the well-being of many of the larger and more conspicuous animals in the garden. Small soil animals like springtails are food for ground-dwelling beetles and spiders, while earthworms are a favourite food of frogs and hedgehogs, and even of larger animals such as foxes and badgers. And don't forget the wildlife that inhabits the compost heap itself.

Decaying organic matter is a favourite haunt of many animals that
would be rare or absent in a garden with no compost heap. Compost
is a favoured habitat for slow worms, one of the few animals in the
garden that really like eating slugs.

A compost heap is a complete ecosystem, a world in
miniature. Worms eat decaying vegetation and excrete organic
compounds that enrich the mix, while their burrowing helps
to aerate the compost. As organic matter is passed through an
earthworm's digestive system, it is finely ground and neutralized
by calcium carbonate that is secreted by the worm's gizzard.

Millipedes, slugs, snails, and woodlice shred the plant
materials, creating more surface area for fungi and bacteria to
work on. Fly larvae (maggots) tunnel through the heap, eating
everything in their path.

Fungi and actinomycetes (a group of organisms intermediate
between bacteria and true fungi) get to work on the tougher plant
residues that the bacteria leave behind. The microbes are food for
organisms such as mites, nematodes, and springtails, which are in
turn eaten by centipedes, ground beetles, rove beetles, spiders,
and more exotic predators such as pseudoscorpions.

Finally larger carnivores (for example slow
worms, hedgehogs, shrews, and toads) move in,
attracted by the warm, sheltered environment
and the abundance of food.

Millipedes process and eat rotting plant material.

Compost basics

People write college theses on compost, but don't let that worry you – all the science you need to know is in the next twelve pages. Essentially, the perfect compost heap needs the right mix of ingredients, plenty of water (but not too much), warmth, and lots of air.

A BALANCED DIET

Ultimately, animals and micro-organisms that turn plant material into compost need to eat the same things that you do. They need energy, most conveniently supplied by carbohydrates. In your case, this means starch and sugars from bread, potatoes, rice, and fruit. The main carbohydrate in plants is cellulose – you can't break this down, but compost micro-organisms can. They also need nitrogen and phosphorus, to make proteins and other vital molecules.

Carbohydrates contain carbon, which provides energy and is the main structural element of living organisms. In practice, anything that contains plenty of nitrogen usually also has lots of phosphorus and other essential elements. A useful, shorthand way to describe compost ingredients is therefore by referring to their carbon:nitrogen, or C:N, ratio.

To understand why this ratio needs to be correct, a useful analogy is your own diet. Without even thinking about it, you aim to eat a balance of these two crucial elements: meat sauce and pasta; fish and chips; cheese and bread; burger and fries; roast beef and roast potatoes.

You know that the perfect sandwich contains more bread than ham or peanut butter and, in a similar fashion, your compost heap needs more carbon than nitrogen.

Some C:N ratios

- poultry manure has a C:N ratio of only 6
- vegetable kitchen waste is about 15
- grass clippings average around 20
- tree leaves are about 50
- straw hovers around 80
- wood and paper are much higher at anything from 100 to 500

This means that, for example, that grass mowings are relatively nitrogen-rich, whereas wood is mostly carbon.

So what is the ideal C:N ratio to aim for when building a compost heap?

Given the importance of nitrogen for making proteins, you might think you should aim to use only stuff with the lowest possible C:N ratio as ingredients in your compost heap. This opinion might be reinforced by learning that the micro-organisms that do most of the work in the compost heap have a C:N ratio between four and nine (people have a similar ratio).

However, as we'll see (*pages 28–29*), nitrogen-rich material on its own has some unfortunate implications for the air supply to your compost heap. Moreover, bacteria don't just need a C:N ratio suitable for turning into more bacteria: much of the carbon in their food is simply "burned", or respired, away as carbon dioxide (CO_2). In fact, about two-thirds of the carbon consumed by bacteria is given off as CO_2, so

the ideal C:N ratio is somewhere around 30.

Because so much carbon is lost during composting, a heap that starts off with a C:N ratio of 30 will deliver finished compost with a ratio around 10 or 15. Comparing the ideal ratio of 30 with the values for various compost materials, it's easy to see that it's a good idea to mix some low-nitrogen, woody stuff in with the lawn mowings and kitchen waste.

However, there's another, even better reason to mix some low-nitrogen waste into your compost heap, because even for bacteria, there is more to life than food. Bacteria have to breathe too, which will bring us to the next basic principle of composting.

A balanced diet for your heap, of roughly three parts soft, green waste to one part woody stuff, will give you rich, dark compost.

YOU CAN'T HAVE TOO MUCH AIR

Composting is an aerobic process, which is a fancy way of saying it needs air. What's more, air is probably even more important than food – the average compost heap runs out of air long before it runs out of food. If there isn't enough air, decomposition becomes anaerobic, which is bad news for two reasons. First, it's much slower than aerobic composting, and second, some of the products, such as ammonia and hydrogen sulphide, don't smell very nice.

Traditional advice is to turn compost heaps, specifically to introduce more air, but the perceived need to turn heaps regularly is enough to put many gardeners off the whole idea of composting. Which brings us to a central dilemma: nitrogen-rich materials such as annual weeds and kitchen waste decompose quickly, but lack structural strength. As soon as they begin decomposing, they lose what little structure they have and collapse into an airless, smelly mess.

It's easy to add materials with more fibre, such as tree and hedge prunings, and these will stop the heap from collapsing. But they decompose much more slowly than soft material, so you end up with coarse, twiggy compost. Shredding woody waste first helps it to break down more quickly, but reduces its usefulness in imparting structure to the heap.

Why does woody waste decompose so slowly? Because it has a high C:N ratio and the composting bacteria are not very good at breaking it down. Fungi are much better, but work only slowly and usually don't like quite the same conditions as bacteria, so a heap that's just right for bacteria will be less good for fungi. Nevertheless, fungi can play an important role in making leafmould (*see pages 88–93*).

So the would-be composter is faced with a dilemma – in fact, two dilemmas for the price of one: how to give the heap structure and what to do with large quantities of woody waste. We'll deal with the woody waste problem later (*see pages 46–47*), but to add structure, we need a material that has some structure but breaks down relatively quickly. One excellent solution is a waste material that every household produces in abundance and is recycled far less often than it should be: paper and cardboard.

Waste paper is the answer to a composter's prayer.

JUST ENOUGH WATER

Soil animals and micro-organisms need water. The bacteria and other microbes live in the film of water that covers compost particles, and most soil animals – especially worms, the most important ones – are very intolerant of drying out. So obviously the ideal compost heap needs to be at least moist. But not too moist – too much water conflicts with the need for air, and there is no faster route to a smelly, anaerobic compost heap than waterlogging.

The ideal water content for rapid composting is about 50–60 per cent by weight, but knowing that isn't very helpful, is it? In practice, this is the water content of a well-wrung sponge. How does this prescription square with the water content of typical compost materials? "Not very well" is the answer.

Kitchen waste and grass clippings are at least 80 per cent water, so a heap made entirely from such materials would be too wet, which would contribute to a lack of oxygen. You could solve the problem by adding drier, woody waste, shredded or otherwise, but this would slow things down too much.

The solution once more is paper and cardboard, which not only lowers the average water content of the heap, but also soaks up the liquid that is released as the softer materials start to decompose.

If you take a handful
from the centre of your heap
and you can **squeeze just
a few drops** of moisture out of it,
that's perfect.

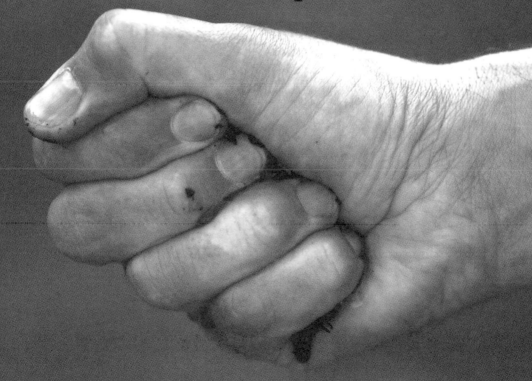

THE CALCIUM FACTOR

The basic story of compost emphasizes the carbon: nitrogen ratio, and rightly so – this has to be at least nearly right, or nothing will work very well. However, the C:N ratio is far from the whole story, and there is one element that has not been given quite the attention it deserves: calcium.

Why might calcium be important in the compost heap? One product of the breakdown of organic matter by bacteria is organic acids. In a well-aerated compost heap, these organic acids are themselves broken down in the later stages of the composting

Acid-loving plants, such as this heather, prefer soils with a low pH.

Most plants, like these herbaceous perennials, grow best in neutral soils.

pH 4 to 6: acid soil

pH 6 to 7: slightly acid to neutral soil

process, but if there is any shortage of oxygen, they can begin to accumulate, making the compost acidic. This is a problem because bacteria do not like acid conditions at all.

The pH scale measures acidity or alkalinity, and goes from 1 (very acid) to 14 (highly alkaline). Pure water has a pH of 7 and is described as neutral. Soil pH depends on geology and climate: acid rocks, like granite or sandstone, and high rainfall result in acid soil; calcium-rich limestone and low rainfall lead to alkaline soil. A soil pH of 6 to 7 is ideal for most plants, but there are some specialized species that grow best on acid or alkaline soils. Few plants thrive on soils with a pH of less than 4 or more than 8.

A roughly neutral pH is perfect for composting bacteria, but they are happy in alkaline conditions, up to pH 8.5. Which is why

Alkaline-tolerant plants, such as lavender, thrive in high-pH soils.

pH 7 to 8: alkaline soil

Leaves that are low in nitrogen and calcium, like those of larch and this pine, make truly awful compost.

materials containing calcium are great for the heap. An acid soil can easily be corrected by adding garden lime (ground limestone), but there is no simple way of making an alkaline soil more acid. If your compost heap is acid because of poor aeration, it's far better to treat the cause rather than attempt to treat the symptoms by adding lime. However, although most green waste contains plenty of calcium, some compost materials are naturally low in calcium.

For example, autumn leaves of oak and hornbeam are relatively rich – for tree leaves – in nitrogen, yet do not make good compost, which makes sense when you discover that both are low in calcium. Woody waste such as hedge prunings, especially of conifers, is also short of calcium, so here there is a case for adding lime to help it break down.

The correlation isn't perfect, but materials that are high in calcium also tend to be high in nitrogen, and no low-calcium materials contain more than moderate levels of nitrogen.

High in calcium Annual and perennial weeds; brassica leaves and stalks; kitchen vegetable waste; leaves of ash, cherry, elm, hawthorn, lime, maple, and rose; seaweed.

Low in calcium Bark, bracken and ferns generally; conifer needles; hay and straw; leaves of beech, birch, hornbeam, and oak; moss; wood.

Compost ingredients

Making compost is like cookery: the secret is in the correct ingredients, plus knowing what to leave out. But don't worry – unlike baking a cake, getting the proportions right is not critical, baking time is up to you, and rubbish ingredients are a positive advantage.

... FROM YOUR HOUSE

The house, and particularly the kitchen, is a major source of compost ingredients. Any green (or orange or yellow or purple) vegetable waste may go on the compost heap. Do not be put off by the tough appearance of things like grapefruit skins – they will compost just as quickly as any other vegetable matter. There's also no problem with left-over, cooked vegetables.

Theoretically, waste meat or fish (cooked or uncooked) can also be composted, but your compost bin must be proof against animals. In practice, it's quite hard to construct a compost bin that cannot be penetrated by a determined rat.

Anything that used to be alive can be composted.

What goes in Coffee grounds, old cotton, silk, or wool clothing (torn up), eggshells, floor sweepings, hair and nail clippings, paper and cardboard, rabbit or hamster bedding, tea bags, vacuum-cleaner dust, vegetable waste, wood ash.

What stays out Cat or dog litter, coke and coal ash, dairy products, disposable nappies, fish and meat waste, oil or fats.

Most types of paper and card make excellent compost ingredients. Large quantities of flat paper should be avoided, and in any case are more suitable for conventional recycling. However, such materials may be used in moderation if you are short of other types of waste paper – printing inks no longer contain toxic heavy metals.

Better for compost are those types of paper that are harder to recycle, such as used tissues and cereal boxes. Birthdays are bonanza times for the serious composter, with all that wrapping paper and bunting. Card with laminated plastic should be avoided: the card will compost okay, but you will have the annoying job of fishing the plastic out of the finished compost.

And if you're alarmed by media stories of identity theft and are worried about what to do with all those old bank statements and credit-card bills, here's the perfect solution – compost them.

What goes in Cardboard packaging, discarded Christmas crackers, egg boxes, old greetings cards, shredded documents, toilet-roll middles, used tissues and kitchen towels, waxed paper, wrapping paper.

What stays out Laminated card such as juice and milk cartons, large quantities of newspaper, telephone directories, very shiny magazines.

... FROM YOUR GARDEN

All normal green garden waste can be composted – after all, disposing of such material is one of the main reasons for composting in the first place. Nearly all of it can go on the compost heap without any treatment, but tough stuff like brassica stalks should first be chopped up, or smashed, with a club hammer or spade. The same goes for tough kitchen waste such as corn cobs.

What about weed seeds? Well, they are not such a serious problem. Even a classic, hot compost heap never achieved a 100 per cent kill, so gardeners have always had to live with weed seeds in compost. Of course, the best defence is vigilance in the first place, so that weeds end up on the compost heap before they get round to setting seed.

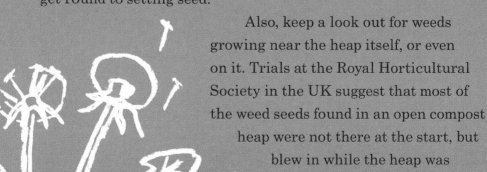

Also, keep a look out for weeds growing near the heap itself, or even on it. Trials at the Royal Horticultural Society in the UK suggest that most of the weed seeds found in an open compost heap were not there at the start, but blew in while the heap was rotting down.

A good bash with a hammer
easily cures the tendency
of tough, fibrous stalks
and corn cobs
to rot slowly.

The problem of weed seeds is
often exaggerated –
a long spell in a compost heap will see off many seeds.

If you adopt the preferred method of composting described later (*see pages 72–75*), which depends very much on worm activity, most of your compost heap will have passed through one or more worms before you use it. Some seeds pass through worms unscathed, but many do not.

Roots or rhizomes of perennial weeds, such as dandelions, docks, and couch grass, are another problem. As far as they are concerned, a compost heap closely resembles their usual, under-ground habitat, so they are not damaged at all by a cool compost heap. The secret here is to kill them before they go on the heap.

There's more than one way of killing a perennial weed, but I think the best is to lay them somewhere dry and sunny until they are thoroughly shrivelled. A more satisfying solution, if you don't have very many weeds, is to bash them thoroughly with a hammer first. Other messier or slower solutions are to drown them in a bucket of water for six weeks or asphyxiate them in a sealed bin liner for a year.

Bake to death perennial weeds before throwing them on your compost heap.

TRICKY STUFF

Some types of garden waste require caution. One of the undoubted virtues of "hot" composting is that weed seeds and pathogens are killed. But traditional, hot composting is hard to achieve in the average garden, so what do we do with such problematic ingredients? Fungal and bacterial pathogens are the worst, but we do need to keep a sense of perspective.

Pests and diseases that live on leaves and stems don't enjoy life in the compost heap, so you don't need to lose much sleep over them. Mildew and black spot are unlikely to survive a long spell in the average compost heap. On the other hand, most soil pests are quite at home in the heap, and are all too likely to survive and be spread around the garden, as are overwintering diseases. There really is no alternative to keeping material with these problems out of the compost heap.

Not very satisfactory solutions are to burn them or bury them in an unused corner of the garden. It's better to add them to a habitat pile, a heap of miscellaneous woody waste intended primarily to provide a wildlife habitat.

When looking at the examples listed opposite, bear in mind that they are for guidance only: no list could possibly be complete, and most available advice on what can be safely composted is anecdotal and contradictory. Also, the longer a heap is left, the smaller is the chance of anything horrible surviving. And last but not least, beneficial microbes in mature garden compost are quite effective at controlling many common diseases. But,

if in doubt, leave it out.

What goes in Material damaged by aphids, black spot, brown rot on fruits, canker, grey mould, leaf miners, leaf mites, mildews, potato blight, sawfly larvae.

What stays out Material that might harbour carrot or cabbage root fly pupae, clubroot of brassicas, eelworms and their eggs, honey fungus, pests that overwinter in soil such as pear midge grubs, root rots of beans and peas, rusts, and viral diseases.

WOODY GARDEN WASTE

Larger gardens, especially those with long hedges, can generate huge quantities of woody waste. We'll consider what to do with it later, but why is it a particular problem?

First, prunings, hedge trimmings, and woody material generally have a high C:N ratio, so are high in carbon and low in nitrogen. This in itself slows down decomposition, but that's only half the problem. The other half is that cellulose is only one of the carbon-rich materials in plants. Another, which may make up 20–30 per cent of wood, is lignin. Lignin's chief disadvantage is that composting bacteria are not good at breaking it down.

Second, woody waste has much bigger stems than green waste, so has a low surface area compared to its volume. This doesn't give bacteria and other organisms much to work on.

The third problem is the exact opposite of that afflicting a pile of grass clippings, which collapses and runs out of air. A pile of raw prunings, on the other hand, contains far too much air, and dries out too quickly. For some gardeners, these problems seem so intractable that composting doesn't look like a serious option. But

don't worry,

there are plenty of environmentally-friendly ways to deal with even a mountain of woody prunings (*see pages 78–87*).

ACTIVE INGREDIENTS

Compost activators are materials intended to make up some deficiency – usually of nitrogen – in the compost heap. Some proprietary compost activators claim to contain micro-organisms, but there should be plenty of these in the compost heap anyway. Direct contact between your heap and the soil will speed up colonization of the heap by bacteria and soil animals. To be absolutely sure, add a spadeful of soil or compost from an existing heap. Cheapest and best of all activators is human urine, applied directly or diluted and added via a watering can.

Something all activators contain is nitrogen. However, if you follow the high-fibre method (*see pages 72–75*), your heap will already have the right carbon:nitrogen (C:N) ratio and no extra nitrogen will be required. If your compost heap does contain too much nitrogen, the excess will simply be broken down and lost as gaseous nitrogen or – worse still – as ammonia, causing

a nasty smell.

However, if you are composting low-nitrogen material such as hedge prunings or autumn leaves, extra nitrogen will probably speed things up. We'll consider the best way to add this when we look at the practicalities of making compost (*see pages 87 and 91*).

As we've seen, many compost materials that lack nitrogen are also low in calcium, and some proprietary activators do contain garden lime. Again, the high-fibre heap doesn't require extra calcium, but the breakdown of naturally acidic materials like woody waste, autumn leaves, and (especially) conifer prunings will be accelerated by the addition of lime.

Good activators Ammonium sulphate (cheapest option); comfrey leaves or liquid feed made from comfrey (organic); dried blood (organic); lime (ground limestone); nettle leaves; fresh or pelleted poultry manure (organic); proprietary activator; spadeful of soil or compost; urine.

WHAT ELSE CAN YOU USE?

The principal goal of composting is to recycle organic matter on the spot, without the awful waste of energy involved in moving it around the country first. Therefore, imported materials should not be added routinely to the compost heap. On the other hand, if there are local sources of composting ingredients that are available cheaply, or perhaps even free, it would be foolish to ignore them.

If your organic waste goes to a local composting scheme, it will be composted at a high temperature under controlled conditions. The resulting compost will be a clean, safe, weed-free material that can be bought and used straightaway in the garden. However, in common with other commercial soil conditioners that are based on recycled garden or forestry waste, it tends to be slightly alkaline, so is not suitable for use around rhododendrons or other acid-loving plants.

Strawy stable manure can go straight on the garden,

while chicken manure is high in nutrients and makes an excellent compost activator. Pigeon manure, often available even in the centre of big cities, is similar.

Many other sources of organic matter are useful if available locally, including bracken, sawdust, seaweed, spent hop waste and mushroom compost, and straw. All these can go straight on the garden as a mulch and will help to improve the soil structure. Bear in mind, however, that in terms of nutrient content and other properties, these materials are very different.

Points to ponder
- mushroom compost is alkaline
- dead bracken, sawdust, and straw contain virtually no nutrients
- material from farms may have had pesticides used on them: always check and, if it has, compost it well before putting it on the garden
- landowners are often happy for you to collect bracken, but always ask first
- collect only loose seaweed washed up by the tide – do not, whatever you do, remove live seaweed from rocks

Useful materials are (*from top, clockwise*) poultry manure, spent hop waste, used mushroom compost, bedding from rabbit and hamster cages.

Sorting your stuff

The lists opposite are a reminder of most of the sorts of things that you might want to compost, divided into (1) soft, nitrogen-rich, (2) moderately nitrogen-rich, and (3) tough, carbon-rich material. Bearing in mind the ideal C:N ratio of 30 for composting, a heap made entirely of rich stuff will have too much nitrogen and one entirely of tough stuff will have too little, so always try to mix the two.

Ingredients: (*from left*) old cut flowers (rich stuff), young hedge clippings (middling stuff), and straw (tough stuff).

Rich stuff (C:N ratio of 5–25) Annual weeds, coffee grounds, comfrey, feathers, general kitchen waste, hair, lawn mowings, nettles, old cut flowers, pigeon manure, pond weed, poultry manure (raw or pelleted), seaweed, pure wool or silk clothing (shredded), soft, green garden waste, urine.

Middling stuff (C:N ratio of 25–50) Brassica and other fibrous, green stems, citrus skins, cotton rags, eggshells (rich in calcium), soiled bedding from hamsters, rabbits, guinea pigs (not dog or cat litter), spent hop waste, tea bags, used potting compost, vacuum cleanings (but not if you have synthetic carpets), waste from distilling, well-rotted cow/horse/pig/sheep manure, wool shoddy, young hedge clippings and soft prunings.

Tough stuff (C:N ratio of 50–600) Bracken, cardboard, corn cobs (crushed), hay or straw, leaves of broad-leaved trees and shrubs, leaves of conifers, nutshells, paper, sawdust, tough hedge clippings, waxed paper, wood ash (rich in potash), wood shavings, woody prunings.

Bacteria like it hot

All biological reactions take place faster at higher temperatures, and composting is no exception. Your heap will turn into compost much more quickly in summer than in winter. If you live in a climate with severe winters, your compost heap will effectively stop completely during the coldest part of the year. Nor are all summers the same. Compost heaps work faster in Madrid or Montreal than in Manchester.

Especially in cool climates like the UK, you will make compost faster in a sheltered, sunny spot, rather than somewhere cool and shady or windy and exposed. In a sunny spot, a black compost bin will work faster than a light-coloured one.

Compost also generates its own heat. A freshly constructed compost heap contains an abundance of food, water, and air. Faced with this bounty, bacteria grow and respire at a prodigious rate. All this activity generates a lot of heat and the temperature of the compost heap rises.

If it gets above about 45°C (113°F), the bacteria that live at everyday temperatures (mesophiles) will be replaced by thermophilic, or heat-loving, bacteria that can continue to thrive to 70°C (158°F) or even beyond. It is one of life's little mysteries that thermophilic bacteria, which cannot grow at all at normal temperatures, are nevertheless everywhere, just waiting for you to make a compost heap.

The keen composter regards such high temperatures as a very good thing

for a variety of reasons. Such temperatures produce finished compost more quickly, and they are high enough to kill weed seeds and disease spores.

A compost heap will always be hotter in the centre and, as the bacteria there begin to run out of food and air, turning the heap adds more air and also mixes in the less-composted, outer parts of the heap, setting off the whole process again. A large, frequently turned heap can stay at a high temperature for a surprisingly long time.

Don't worry, by the way, that this heat is bad for other compost heap inhabitants. Mesophilic bacteria survive as resistant spores, and mobile animals (beetles, centipedes, worms, and so on) simply move to the outer parts of the heap until things start to cool down.

So much for theory.

Size does matter: only huge heaps get really hot.

To see how easy it is for the average gardener to achieve high composting temperatures, the Royal Horticultural Society (RHS) in the UK set up a trial of different sizes of compost bins and heaps at their garden at Wisley.

The trial heaps were

- a standard, slatted, wooden bin bought from a large DIY chain store, with a volume of 0.75 cubic metre (26 cu.ft)
- a typical, local authority plastic bin, of 0.3 cubic metre (11 cu.ft)
- an open heap, also sized about 0.3 cubic metre (11 cu.ft)

All contained the same mix of typical garden waste: large, woody material was chipped and smaller material was shredded. The trial was started in late autumn: although the weather at this time is too cold to be ideal for compost-making, it is one of the few times that many gardeners will have a large quantity of waste material available.

The trial heaps were compared with the main heap at the RHS Garden, Wisley, which is enormous – at least 30 cubic metres (1,060 cu.ft). Despite air temperatures below 10°C (50°F), the temperature of this heap quickly rose to around 70°C (158°F).

After two weeks, the heap was turned and the cold air admitted briefly reduced its temperature to below 50°C (122°F). But it was soon back up to over 60°C (140°F) again, and remained above 50°C, with monthly turning, for several months.

No such luck for the trial heaps. None ever achieved more than a few degrees above air temperature, with or without turning. Probably because of its larger size and better insulation, the wooden bin was the best of a bad bunch, and the plastic bin was slightly warmer than the open heap. Crucially however, none got anywhere near a temperature that would kill disease pathogens or weed seeds. So much for the bad news.

The good news is that after a year, whether turned or not, all the heaps produced perfectly good compost.

However, the compost from the open heap contained more weed seeds than the compost from the bins. It also had lower levels of plant nutrients, probably because they had been washed out by rain.

Making compost:
paper, prunings, and patience

Classic composting

The traditional advice for constructing a classic compost heap is quite simple. First, collect together a mixture of soft, nitrogen-rich waste and tougher, carbon-rich material. Shred any tree and shrub prunings.

Second, start filling your compost bin with layers of different materials, adding a spadeful of compost or soil now and then – the right micro-organisms will colonize your heap eventually anyway, but there's no harm in giving them a helping hand. Carry on until your heap measures at least one cubic metre (1 cu.yd), or more if possible. If the heap seems dry, water it. Cover it with the bin lid or a piece of old carpet.

Your heap should soon start to get hot. When it starts to cool, turn it and it will heat up again. When it starts to cool again, turn it for a third time, and leave until done.

Sounds simple, doesn't it? Unfortunately, it's this stately home approach that caused generations of gardeners to abandon the whole idea of making compost. In fact, this

apparently simple advice is
riddled with weasel words
that gloss over real difficulties.

"Turn your heap when it starts to cool down."

Modern gardeners are busy people, with their compost heap somewhere near the bottom of their list of priorities. Turning a large compost heap is hard work, and doing it twice sounds like adding insult to injury. There's also the anxiety of whether you've got the timing right. Is it cooling down yet? Have I left it too long?

"Collect together at least a cubic metre of waste."

Pardon?

How often does the owner of a modern, small garden have a cubic metre (cu. yd) of waste at one time? Pause at this point and try to visualize a cubic metre of garden waste (go and get a tape measure if necessary).

"Well then," goes the advice, "gather the materials over a period of time."

OK, but where do you store this stuff while you are waiting to collect enough? An even more interesting question is how you stop the green waste from starting to compost before it goes on the compost heap. Keep it in the fridge maybe?

Something else the books never mention. As described, composting is clearly a batch process, like putting a load in the washing machine. A full load of compost material is assembled and, after a time, finished compost results.

Which raises the awkward question: what do you do with compostable material that accumulates meanwhile? Clearly, if traditional composting is to work at all, you must have at least two compost heaps.

"Fill your compost bin with at least a cubic metre of waste."

Naturally, this assumes that you have a compost bin that will hold that amount. So how big are commercial compost bins? Many retailers sell their own version of the classic, wooden "New Zealand" box; a quick check of catalogues and websites shows that

It's not easy squeezing a cubic metre of waste into most compost bins.

the standard box bin varies from 0.3–0.75 cubic metre (11–26 cu.ft). You can find larger bins, up to 1.3 cubic metres (46 cu.ft), but you have to look quite hard to find them.

Plastic compost bins, of the type often provided free or at a subsidized price by local government, are generally smaller. A leaflet from my local authority lists three bins, ranging from 0.23–0.6 cubic metres (8–21 cu.ft). Fancier options, such as bins disguised as beehives and tumblers, are smaller still. I'm forced to conclude that manufacturers of compost bins do not expect the average gardener to assemble a cubic metre of compost at one go.

"If the heap seems dry, add some water."

This sounds simple enough, but in practice conceals a minefield. We've already seen that moisture content has consequences for aeration (*see pages 28–29*), but there are other, more subtle effects too. All else being equal,

a wet compost heap heats up more slowly than a dry one.

Water is also a much better conductor of heat than air, which is why cold water always feels much colder than air at the same temperature. So a wet compost heap loses heat more quickly than a dry one.

In fact, although this is unlikely to happen to you, spontaneous fires at commercial composting sites are not that uncommon, and are usually caused by a large heap that is (at least in part) too dry. The message is that moisture content is critical: it must be high enough to allow composting to occur, but not so high that heat is lost too quickly. On a domestic scale, the moisture content of a compost heap is difficult to measure or control: quite small variations in moisture content are probably responsible for the rather unpredictable behaviour of the typical heap.

Finally, does it work? That is, if you have survived the assault course needed to assemble a compost heap in the required manner, will it do what it should do? The Royal Horticultural Society research described previously (*see pages 60–61*) plainly shows that it probably won't. The only simple way of ensuring a compost heap gets hot and stays hot is to make it larger than recommended by the books, and certainly larger than a typical compost bin.

It seems clear that classical hot composting was designed by (and for) people with big gardens, plenty of space, and ready access to outside sources of compost materials, typically animal manures. In such gardens, classical composting is still alive and well. At the RHS Garden, Wisley, in the UK, huge quantities of waste are chipped, shredded, and mixed by special machinery, then blended into huge heaps, typically 2×4×12m (6×12×40ft) in size, or about 100 times the minimum recommended size of the domestic heap. This makes excellent compost in about four months, but it's a process the ordinary gardener can only dream about.

Of course, I'm not saying it's impossible to make a traditional, hot compost heap in an average bin. It's just that you will have to take some elaborate precautions, probably including more than one of these steps:

- importing composting material from outside the garden
- trying to make compost only in summer
- installing effective insulation around your bin
- siting the compost bin in the sunniest, most sheltered spot
- moving to somewhere with warmer summers.

At which point, the average gardener could be forgiven for concluding that the game is hardly worth the candle. Gardening is supposed to be fun, after all.

Compost for realists

Woody waste can cause such trouble that I'm going to start out by assuming you don't have any. Later, we will see what can be done with woody waste, but first let's consider what you can do realistically with the soft garden and household waste and lawn mowings.

SOFT WASTE

For the average gardener, the easiest way to cope with most soft waste is to make a "high-fibre" compost heap. The method described here is based on that developed by the Centre for Alternative Technology (CAT) in Wales, in the UK. Green kitchen and garden waste and paper and card are essential ingredients.

Any paper or card you add to a high-fibre heap should be crumpled to make irregular, three-dimensional shapes. Egg boxes and toilet-roll tubes are perfect without any pre-treatment. Start with a layer of paper and card to improve the drainage at the base, then just add paper and green waste as it comes along – no need for any distinct "layering".

The only rules are to make sure that you have approximately equal volumes of paper and green waste, and not to add pure green waste in a layer more than 15cm (6in) deep.

Worms are the key
to this kind of composting

(not earthworms that live in soil, but smaller, related species called brandlings). In fact, this sort of compost heap is essentially a large wormery (*see pages 140–145*), but a lot less trouble. Worms should colonize naturally, but you can make sure by adding some from an existing heap. If you're starting from scratch, get some worms from a compost-friendly neighbour. As a last resort, buy them from compost specialists, but this should not be necessary.

In a high-fibre heap, most of the actual composting activity is confined to a relatively narrow layer, with fresh material above and maturing compost below. If your heap is working well, this narrow layer should be very rich in worms. Since this layer-cake arrangement is vital to the success of your heap, it follows that you need do nothing other than add new material to the top. Certainly

no turning is required.

If you have a bin that allows access to the base of the heap, small quantities of finished compost may be removed from the bottom, but it's far better to leave well alone until the bin is full. Then just remove the undecomposed material and worm-rich layer from the top and tip it straight into a second bin (if you have one), or put it in the original bin after removing the finished compost.

A MOWN ABOUT GRASS CUTTINGS

In many gardens, there may be a huge glut of lawn mowings in the summer. The solution is simply to stockpile surplus cardboard to make sure that you can keep the green waste:paper ratio about equal during these brief periods. If you can't do this, loosely screwed-up, single sheets of newspaper will work just as well. An alternative is simply to use grass clippings as a mulch (*see pages 168–169*).

If you have a large vegetable plot, there might be another glut of soft green material later in the season, when you're disposing of old runner bean, courgette, and tomato plants. This sort of green waste is rarely a problem, since it has more inherent structure than grass clippings.

Crumpled newspaper saves a grassy heap from becoming slimy and smelly.

A KNOTTY PROBLEM

The high-fibre method described in the previous pages is not designed to deal with woody waste or autumn leaves. Nevertheless, try to keep a sense of perspective, and don't panic if you have small quantities of these things. Regular trimmings from a modest privet hedge, or the autumn leaves that fall on your lawn from a tree a couple of gardens away, will probably not upset your high-fibre heap too much.

On the other hand, if you have (like me) sackloads of trimmings from a long beech hedge, your high-fibre heap will not cope. But don't worry, there are many other good ways of dealing with woody waste, listed overleaf in approximately declining order of desirability.

1. Shred and use directly as a mulch.

If you have a shredder, this is the simplest solution (*see pages 82–85*), which avoids completely the difficulty of composting this material. You will read dire warnings about woody mulches releasing toxins or using up all the nitrogen in your soil, but both problems are much exaggerated.

For hedge prunings, an alternative is simply to push them out of the way under the hedge, where they will slowly decompose and also provide an ideal hiding place for hibernating hedgehogs and other garden wildlife.

2. Make a separate compost heap specifically designed for woody waste.

If you do this, you can deal with the tendency of woody waste to rot slowly and dry out, by treating it slightly differently to general compost. To find out how easy it is to do this, see pages 85–87.

3. Make a habitat pile.

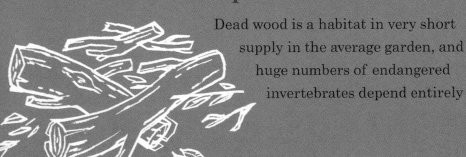

Dead wood is a habitat in very short supply in the average garden, and huge numbers of endangered invertebrates depend entirely on it for their survival. A heap of logs and thicker branches makes a log pile; add smaller, woody stuff and it's a habitat pile. Both are equally good for wildlife. The best option for the wildlife gardener with no shredder, and for any woody waste too thick to be shredded.

4. Let someone else deal with it.

This is a good option if your local authority or waste-disposal company composts garden waste – especially if they are willing to collect it. If they aren't, ask them why not. On the other hand, this is a much less environmentally friendly option if you have to deliver the waste yourself.

5. Burn it.

While I recognize that, for some gardeners, a good bonfire is one of the pleasures of gardening, this does put all the carbon that was fixed in the plant material straight back into the atmosphere. It also squanders most of the value of the waste.

At least you can recycle the wood ash, which contains some potassium (K). In the autumn, build your bonfire immediately before burning it, or at least check for hibernating hedgehogs and other creatures before lighting it. Try not to annoy your neighbours, who may not enjoy bonfires as much as you do. If you have an open fire or suitable stove, burn larger woody waste in the house and return the ash to the garden.

WOOD FOR THE CHOP

If you have a high-fibre compost heap, it will not object to small quantities of woody waste or autumn leaves (especially if they are shredded first). The point at which you decide you have so much of this stuff that you have to find something else to do with it is largely up to you.

Because woody waste breaks down so much more slowly than soft waste, the more you add to your heap, the coarser and more twiggy will be the product. Whether this is a problem depends on exactly what you want your compost for. In the end, it comes down to personal choice. We'll discuss the vexed question of when compost is "ready" later on (*see pages 148–151*).

A lot hinges on whether you own a shredder. This in turn depends on your attitude to cost and the noise (no shredder is exactly quiet), and whether you think you produce enough woody material to justify owning one. If you generate most of your woody waste in one massive, annual burst of hedge-pruning, hiring a shredder is an option. Joining a local gardening club that hires out tools to members is another possibility.

Why is a shredder so important? Shredding can't improve the chemical composition of woody waste, but it does smash it into small, jagged, irregular pieces, hugely increasing the area that bacteria and other micro-organisms have to work on. Shredding

Composting woody waste is **not as impossible as it appears**, especially if you shred it first.

also significantly reduces the volume of a pile of prunings and counters the tendency of raw prunings to dry out too quickly.

Really "green" gardeners object to the energy used by shredders, but this is trivial compared to all the other energy used by modern living. Running a shredder for half an hour will deal with 50kg (110lb) of prunings and uses about as much electricity as watching television for an evening.

If you have a shredder, modest quantities of shredded, woody material may be added to a high-fibre compost heap. They will still break down more slowly than the soft wastes, but the smaller

Before shredding, a heap of woody prunings takes up a lot of space.

woody pieces will make the finished product look better. Large quantities of shredded woody waste may simply be piled up in their own heap and will be broken down rather slowly by fungi, eventually producing something very like leafmould.

Unshredded woody waste can be treated in exactly the same way as shredded, but will take an extremely long time to break down. In fact, sticks or stems thicker than 2cm (¾in) will take so long to rot that composting is not a realistic option – the habitat pile or the bonfire are best for this larger stuff. To speed things up, you need to address the tendency of woody waste to dry out.

After shredding, the prunings are dramatically reduced in volume.

This means it needs to go in a closed bin, ideally taller than it is wide, so that its own weight tends to compress it and reduce the large air spaces. It also helps to add other things that will help to fill in the spaces, such as old potting compost and soil. When you pull up weeds, don't knock any of the soil off the roots: just add the whole lot to the heap. The good thing about a heap like this is that it will take anything not suitable for the high-fibre compost heap – including autumn leaves.

Shredded or not, woody waste has a high carbon:nitrogen (C:N) ratio, so will benefit from judicious additions of activators containing nitrogen (*see pages 48–49*). Woody material, like many autumn leaves, also tends to be low in calcium, so a handful of garden lime (ground limestone) helps too. Lime is especially good if you have many conifer prunings, which tend to be very acid.

Finally, the chief necessities for composting woody waste are patience and space.

Shredded woody material with added activators should make decent compost in a year, but on its own may take two years, while unshredded material may take three years. This means you will always have two or three heaps underway at any time, so you'll need room to accommodate these. Fortunately, the gardens that produce large quantities of woody waste are most likely to be those with space to deal with it.

RAKING THEM IN

The traditional advice on composting tree leaves is clear and unambiguous: don't bother. Leaves from trees are low in nitrogen and calcium and high in carbon, especially in tough, indigestible stuff like lignin (the main component of wood) and tannins, so they are best kept away from the compost heap.

Yet not all tree leaves are the same, and the usual advice is founded on the assumption that gardeners can't tell them apart. The real story, for gardeners who can tell them apart, is that leaves of some trees are tough and slow to break down. However, other leaves are much richer in nitrogen and calcium and make a useful addition to the compost heap.

Good leaves Ash, cherry, elm, lime (linden or basswood), maple, poplar (cottonwood), willow.

Bad leaves Beech, birch, hornbeam, oak, sweet chestnut.

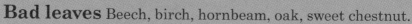

By far the best tool
for raking leaves off a lawn is
a spring-tined rake.
Don't waste money on
a powered leaf-blower or vacuum.

If your tree identification is not up to scratch, there's an easy way to tell good, more readily compostable, leaves from slower-rotting ones.

Leaves are shed by some species of trees while still green; you can add them to the heap in moderate quantities.

Red or yellow leaves may be used in small amounts.

Brown leaves should be avoided in the mixed compost heap, but they do make good leafmould (*see overleaf*).

Although all tree leaves have some structure and won't collapse in the same way as grass clippings do, avoid adding leaves in thick layers that will end up as wet, airless slabs. If it looks like the volume of leaves may cause a problem, mix them with paper and card as for green waste.

Beech, oak, and other brown tree leaves break down very slowly, unless they are chopped and mixed with more nitrogen-rich material. An excellent way of doing this, especially if your lawn is covered with leaves, is to run the mower over both grass and leaves. All leaves will compost more quickly if shredded in this way. The shredded leaf-and-grass mixture may be added to the compost heap in moderation, or applied directly as a mulch.

In fact, leaves would make a good mulch on their own, if they didn't blow around so easily.

By the way, take care when collecting autumn leaves to make leafmould. Drifts of dry leaves are favourite sites for hibernating hedgehogs. If you're not sure that the leaves under your hedge are uninhabited, leave well alone.

An alternative, and the only option if you have a lot of the wrong kind of leaves, is to

quarantine them
in their own heap
and make leafmould.

You may be told to stack leaves in a wire cage or in black, plastic sacks. If these two pieces of advice seem contradictory, that's because making leafmould doesn't need any special conditions at all. Simply stack leaves in a heap, water, and leave – preferably for about two years. During this time, decomposition will be caused mainly by fungi, which are not deterred by acidic conditions and secrete enzymes that break down lignin.

The only reason to stack leaves in a wire cage is to stop them blowing away. Why a wire cage rather than a compost bin? Because it's cheaper, but you can use a compost bin if you like.

The only reason to stack leaves in plastic sacks is that it's a cheap way to keep them moist in dry weather. As long as you're happy to water your heap if the surface looks very dry, a wire cage will be fine.

Tooling up

For adding material from a wheelbarrow, removing finished compost, and turning a heap (if you insist), a garden fork, ideally stainless steel, is the perfect tool. For the serious composter, planning to deal with large quantities of waste and finished compost, a wheelbarrow is another must.

A bucket is almost too universally useful to be described merely as a compost tool. Use it for transferring kitchen waste and weeds to the heap and for distributing small quantities of finished compost around the garden. The plastic tub trugs now available are just as handy. Secateurs are essential for chopping up tough plant stems or small amounts of woody stuff.

Other useful, but far from essential, tools include a shredder and tools for chopping and smashing tough waste – an axe, club hammer, or long-handled loppers. A soil sieve comes in handy if you want to use garden compost to make your own potting compost.

Few tools are absolutely essential to compost-making, but **a garden or compost fork** comes as close as anything.

Compost bins: wood, wire, and worms

Why have a bin?

In truth, you don't need a bin to make compost. An open heap will compost eventually, and there isn't much evidence that it takes a great deal longer than a bin or produces inferior compost. Nonetheless, there are several reasons for using a bin rather than a heap.

Open heap or bin?

- any weed seeds blowing around will tend to accumulate in an open heap, but not in a bin
- rain will wash essential plant nutrients out of an open heap – a covered bin will not suffer such leaching
- weed and leaching problems could be solved by covering a heap with plastic sheeting or some old carpet
- compost in a bin will be warmer than an open heap, although the difference will be slight unless you go to unusual lengths to insulate your bin
- an open heap takes up more room, and the surface tends to dry out and blow around or be scattered by animals
- the high-fibre method (*see pages 72–75*) also works better in a bin, since it's hard to maintain an active layer that is full of worms in an open heap

In practice,
the main reason for using a bin
is simple tidiness.

Nevertheless, keep the issue of bins in perspective. The correct mix of materials will compost satisfactorily with or without a bin, and no bin will persuade unshredded hedge prunings to compost quickly. For most gardeners, the choice of bin should be dictated largely by considerations of cost and convenience.

Choosing a bin

Your local authority or waste-disposal company may provide compost bins for little more than the cost of delivery, or even completely free. (This appears to be remarkably altruistic, but everything you compost is something they don't have to collect and dispose of.) If they do supply bins, this is almost certainly your best bet.

Small hatches make it difficult to get stuck in with a fork when the compost is ready.

For example, in my locality, householders are provided with a choice of three plastic bins, from 226 to 600 litre (50 to 132 gallon) capacity. Each costs around ten per cent of what they would cost at a garden centre or shop. Which is the one for you?

Some plastic bins are one-piece, truncated cones with a removable lid, while others require some very simple assembly. If you doubt your ability to assemble anything and the words "flat pack" send a shiver down your spine, a one-piece bin is for you. One-piece bins also tend to be more sturdy. Otherwise (and this applies to other types of bin too),

it's mainly a question of size and access.

None of the typical bins on the market is large enough to produce "hot" compost reliably, so there's no need to worry on that score. Choose a bin that's big enough, but not too big, bearing in mind the quantity of material you're likely to produce, the space the bin takes up, and whether you want more than one bin.

The ideal bin would stop moisture escaping and let air in. In practice, these two aims are incompatible: keeping in moisture is more important. So don't buy or make a bin with holes in the sides. These allow compost at the edges to dry out, leading to an annoying mixture of decomposed material in the centre and undecomposed material round the edges.

PLASTIC FANTASTIC

The simplest and smallest plastic bins are formed from one moulded piece of plastic, with a lid. Waste material goes in at the top and, to get at the finished compost, you lift off the whole bin. Although some plastic bins are green, the free or cheap ones tend to be black. For those gardeners who object to plastic bins on environmental grounds, it's usually possible to get bins made of recycled plastic. There are other points that you may want to consider:

Check whether the hole at the top is big enough. Emptying a bucket into a small hole may not be a problem, but if you produce enough compost material to require a wheelbarrow, trying to fork stuff up and into a small hole might be annoying.

Make sure that the top of the bin is not inconveniently high for you.

Most bins (including the free ones) have a lid that simply lifts off, but you might find a hinged lid more convenient.

Some expensive plastic bins have double walls, but the great majority offer little in the way of insulation, so gardeners in cold climates should consider wooden, wire and cardboard, or straw-bale bins (*see pages 108–121*).

Most plastic bins don't have any holes in them, but a few have slatted sides with quite big gaps between the slats. Many wooden bins are like this too, and both should be avoided. A few small ventilation holes at the base are OK, but that's all. If you already have a holey bin, like the flat-pack bin shown overleaf, you could line it with some cardboard to keep out the draughts.

Also consider whether you will want to retrieve compost from the base of the bin. If you do, you need a bin with a hatch at the base. Larger bins may have two or even four hatches, allowing access from any side, but smaller ones usually have a single hatch (*see overleaf*).

Simple flat-pack bin, lined with cardboard (*overleaf, left*), and plastic bins (*overleaf, right*).

WOODEN PERFORMANCE

Not all new wooden bins make access as easy as it should be. Beware of lift-off wooden lids, which can become very heavy, especially when wet. A plastic or hinged wooden lid is better. The best designs have a front panel that consists of separate, removable slats, which can be inserted as the bin fills up and removed later for access to the finished product.

One problem with wooden bins is cost. Wooden bins are not inherently more expensive than the plastic ones, but they are rarely available free or at subsidized prices. A new wooden bin can work out quite expensive even if you buy wood to make your own. Untreated, sawn (that is, not planed) timber is cheapest. Treated wood will last much longer, but seriously green gardeners should enquire what is in the wood preservative, since some contain heavy metals or other toxic chemicals.

STACK AND UNPACK IT!

Stacking bins make it easy to build up a heap as well as get to the finished compost. This type of bin is completely portable since you have to lift only one section at a time.

- **To start the heap,** place one section on the ground and begin to fill with compost material. Once it is full, place the next section on top. If your bin has a lid, like this beehive model, put it on top to keep the heap moist. If you have a home-made or open stacking bin, use some other cover. Keep building up the bin, by adding and filling a section at a time.

- **Fill the bin to the top** and then leave it, covered, to rot down for six to nine months. If you wish, you could remove the upper sections of the bin as the compost subsides and start another heap with another cover somewhere else.

- **Unpack the finished heap** simply by lifting off all the sections of the bin. (Beehive models sometimes have a crossbar at the base, so leave the base section in place.) You can then easily shovel up the contents.

STICKING WITH WOOD

Bins made of untreated timber should last for many years. The weak link is often the base, which will rot if it is in contact with permanently damp soil. Standing the bin on bricks, slates, or some broken paving slabs should help. Standard wooden bins are heavy; for a more portable option, try woven hurdles or bins made of stacking sections.

Wooden options: (*from left to right*) hazel hurdle bin, stacking bin, and a bay made from builder's pallets.

DIY is worth a try

If you are fairly competent at DIY, there are lots of materials, apart from plastic and wood, to consider. Bricks or breeze blocks make sturdy, long-lasting compost bins. Breeze blocks are cheap, quick, and easy; they don't look as nice as bricks, but you could paint or grow climbers over them. Both need foundations at least 15cm (6in) deep and twice as wide as the walls of the bin.

Other options include corrugated iron, plastic, or chicken wire, which should be screwed to four stout, wooden posts. Most home-made wooden designs require posts to be driven into the ground. Untreated posts in soil soon rot, but last much longer if they're fixed into metal post supports. Stop the post tops rotting by capping them with wooden finials.

It's not so easy to make these designs with a removable front, but in my experience there's nothing wrong with an open bin, with only three sides. Material falling out of the front shouldn't be a problem as long as it is added carefully but, if it is a bit messy, cover the top and front with a piece of old carpet or sacking.

FINDING A USE FOR IT

For the serious recycler, it's clear that the compost bin itself should be recycled. Fortunately, there is no shortage of suitable materials. Old floorboards, plastic, corrugated iron, old doors, pallets, bricks, builder's bags, and other useful junk are thrown away in ever-increasing quantities – good compost bins can be made from all of them. Ask a local supplier of recycled building materials or just keep an eye on the contents of local skips. My compost bins consist mostly of the remains of some scrapped wardrobes, interspersed with bits of old kitchen units. You may disapprove but, if you think a compost bin should be some kind of fashion statement, you may not be cut out for serious composting.

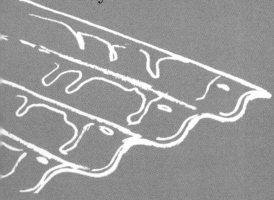

Don't let your old tyres
        moulder in a landfill site –
give them a new lease of life
        as a compost bin.

GET WIRED UP

A cheap, do-it-yourself bin is easy to make from chicken wire by stapling it to four posts and lining it with cardboard. A slightly more complicated version would have two layers of wire, with the gap between them filled in with screwed-up newspaper or sheets of cardboard. The cardboard eventually will rot, but is easily replaced.

- **Knock four 1.5m (5ft) posts** into the ground, about 75cm (30in) apart and 30cm (12in) deep. Use a piece of chicken wire, about 1.2m (4ft) wide and 2.5m (8ft) long, and unroll it around the posts. Fix it securely to the posts with plenty of fencing staples as you go. Leave the front open.

- **Once the wire is fixed** to the fourth post, snip off the excess. Check that no sharp snags of wire are sticking out; trim or bend them back so that they cannot cause injury.

- **Line the insides** of the chicken wire with several layers of flattened cardboard boxes, slotting the boxes in-between the posts and wire to hold them in place. Start building up your compost in the bin. Use a cover to stop the rain soaking the compost material and to keep it warm.

BALING OUT

An unorthodox, but quick, cheap, and simple bin can be made from a few bales. Straw is an excellent insulator, so it's possible to make "hot" compost from relatively small amounts of material in the bin.

Eventually, of course, the bin itself will compost down, but that's not a problem: just buy more bales and start again. The walls of a straw bin take up rather a lot of room, but you can exploit this by planting into the top bales. Anything that needs a rich soil and grows fast will look good, such as bush tomatoes, courgettes, cucumbers, French beans, petunias, squashes, or trailing nasturtiums.

- **Stack six bales,** on their thin sides, to form three walls.

- **Bang in 1.5m (5ft) stakes** snugly against the outsides of the bales, two posts to each side. Insert a 1.5m (5ft) cane at the centre of the inside of each wall. These supports will hold up the bales when they start to decay.

- **Place another bale** against the front of the bin. Start off the heap with material that has a bit of structure, for drainage, such as thin prunings or old bean haulms. As the heap fills up, cover with cardboard, sacking, or old carpet.

- **To plant in the top,** scoop out a small hollow and fill with compost or soil. Straw is pretty dry and has almost no nutrients, so add some fertilizer to the mix and water well.

BAG IT AND BIN IT

With a bit of imagination and the bare minimum of
DIY skills, a remarkable variety of junk can form
the basis of a cheap, or even free, compost bin. The
bin can even be made of compost itself – if you have
a lot of sacks of rotting leaves, use them to build a
circular wall, line it with cardboard, and hey presto!
you have a compost bin in the middle.

Bin walls (*below*) of sacks of leaves.   **Builder's bag** (*right*) on four posts.

Working undercover

I'm convinced that a compost bin needs some kind of lid or cover, whether it is old carpet or cardboard or a purpose-made cover. It helps to retain heat and stops the surface drying out in dry weather. Rain will both cool down an uncovered bin and wash out the nutrients. Having said that, there are dissenting voices.

The Centre for Alternative Technology (CAT), in Wales, recommend that their high-fibre heap (*see pages 72–75*) should be half-covered. The rationale is that this is the best way of making sure that the heap always will provide perfect conditions for the worms on which the system depends. The location of these ideal conditions will move around the heap, depending on the weather, but they will always exist in there somewhere.

Most commercial bins come with a lid anyway but, if you have any choice, bear in mind that the lid should be easy to remove and replace – ideally with one hand – but not so light that it blows off in the wind. Since lids on plastic bins tend to be light, check when buying that any removable plastic lid is a good fit.

Keep a lid on it with a special padded cover (*top left*), sacks (*top right*), or an old blanket (*bottom*).

Tumbler bins

It is claimed that tumbler bins solve the biggest compost problem, which is keeping the mix aerated. In fact, of course, this is one of those problems, like maintaining the correct carbon:nitrogen (C:N) ratio or a suitable pH, that is best solved by having the correct mixture of materials to start with.

The evidence is that tumblers do make decent compost relatively quickly, but not all that much quicker than standard, static bins. Also, the most widely available (and cheapest) design, which turns end-over-end, is awkward to use. Once the compost shrinks a little, it all tends to collect at the bottom, which makes it difficult to turn. Bins that rotate like a toilet roll (*see overleaf*) avoid this problem, but also tend to be very expensive.

Something else to consider before spending a lot of money on one is your level of motivation. If they are to work well, tumbler bins need turning every few days (ideally, every day). Will you do that, or will it turn out like the exercise bike that you promised you would use every day and is now gathering dust in the attic?

You will need **dedication and muscle power** to turn these vertical tumblers **regularly.**

Some tumbler bins are claimed to make compost in 14 days. Maybe so – given the right location, a large quantity of the right material, the right time of year, and a bit of luck. Fourteen-day compost is a major selling point, presented as something any sensible gardener would want. And yet, I can't help wondering why anyone would feel the need to make compost in two weeks.

What's the hurry?

If you're starting from scratch, I can imagine that waiting six, ten, or even twelve months for your first batch of compost might seem a long time. But making and using compost is part of the normal cycle of gardening. However you choose to organize your compost-making, it's axiomatic that once things have been underway for a year or so, compost material goes into the system at the same rate that finished compost comes out at the other end.

The volume of a tumbler bin is anything from 200–600 litres (44–132 gallons), depending on the model. Even if you produce this volume of material every 14 days, which is in practice a tall order, that doesn't mean you need to make compost in a fortnight. That rate of production implies you have a large garden – either that or you own a hotel.

If this is the case, you probably also have enough room for several conventional compost bins, containing compost at various stages of maturity. Alternatively, such a large quantity of waste would allow you to have one or two really large heaps, big enough for genuine, "hot" composting. Large, hot heaps produce finished compost in about four months, with no effort at all.

Am I trying to persuade you not to invest in a tumbler bin? No, but I am suggesting you consider carefully four things:

- the quantity of compost material your garden produces
- how much space you are willing to devote to dealing with it
- how much time and effort you want to spend
- the cost.

The more laissez-faire your approach, and the longer you take to make compost, the more space your compost will occupy (and the less effort required). But you will still make compost in the end!

Location, location

It's important that a compost heap is quickly colonized by beetles, millipedes, worms, and other hungry soil animals. At the same time, you want any liquid that dribbles from the heap to soak into the soil rather than collect in a smelly puddle. Thus one of the few genuinely unbreakable rules of composting is that your bin should be sited on soil, not on a hard surface.

We've touched briefly on how the location of your compost heap will affect its temperature (and therefore how fast it works), but for most gardeners the location of the compost heap is a compromise between aesthetics and convenience.

Few compost heaps are exactly beautiful, so it is tempting to site your heap as far out of the way as possible. Although neither flies nor smells should be a problem with a properly functioning heap, the suspicion that they might be tends to reinforce this inclination.

Remember though that, if your compost heap is too inaccessible, you may be less likely to use it for kitchen waste, especially when it's dark, cold, and raining! Ideally, the compost

heap should be conveniently near both the sources and the final destination of compost materials. This often means it should be near the vegetable plot, if you have one.

For smaller, portable bins, consider not having a fixed location at all. It seems a shame to waste the highly fertile patch that develops directly under the bin, so

why not move
the bin around?

In fact, if you have a vegetable plot, why not simply incorporate a moveable compost bin into a normal crop-rotation cycle? This practice involves growing different crops on any specific patch of soil in a three- or four-year cycle. Just add compost to the cycle.

In reality, some kind of smaller bin is handy for taking household waste from the kitchen to the heap. Whether you keep this kitchen bin indoors or out is up to you. Indoors is more convenient, but you will need to empty it often to make sure that you avoid any problems with flies and smells. Some fancy designs, such as ceramic crocks, or cheaper plastic versions, come with carbon filters that are supposed to stop smells escaping.

My personal preference is for a bin located just outside the back door. A simple bucket is cheap and convenient if you have somewhere under cover to put it. A welcome innovation is the biodegradable "plastic" bag, made from corn, or maize, starch. Line your kitchen bin with one of these, then just put the whole lot on the compost heap.

How many bins?

It would be presumptuous of me to offer detailed prescriptions as to how you should organize your compost-making. After all, every garden is different, with a unique combination of quantities and proportions of soft and tough garden, and kitchen, waste. Every gardener is different too, with very different levels of commitment to compost-making and to recycling in general.

In a sense, things are easier in a large garden, where there is enough material in several, distinct "waste streams" to merit their own specialist treatment. Also, there is plenty of space.

The large garden might have a high-fibre bin to deal with kitchen waste, paper, and some grass clippings, as well as two "long-stay" bins full of shredded prunings, hedge trimmings,

autumn leaves, spent compost, and other garden waste. You might have one or more separate bins for leafmould, and maybe even one to deal with gluts of lawn mowings.

In reality, most gardeners live in towns and cities, and most urban gardens are relatively small. Here, most waste is soft (grass clippings, kitchen scraps, annual weeds, old bedding plants), but there's usually an irritating trickle of tougher material.

This is enough to interfere with the proper functioning of a pure, high-fibre heap, but not really enough to justify separate

Ingeniously designed bins of recycled plywood and window frames, with sliding front panels.

treatment. Certainly not enough to warrant the purchase of a shredder. The best solution may be to accept that you're never going to produce compost very quickly and to have two bins, into which you put everything except the largest, woody material.

Once one bin is full, simply leave it for a year while you fill the other bin.

This "two all-purpose bins" system works well, as long as you make sure that each bin is big enough to take a year's waste without it overflowing. Because the compost includes some woody waste, the finished product is always a bit twiggy, but that shouldn't be a problem.

Material that's too tough to compost can be pushed under a hedge or made into a habitat pile in an out-of-the-way corner. If there's too much of the tough stuff, take or send it to your local community composting scheme.

This is essentially the system that operates in my garden, with two additions. My garden is surrounded by a tall beech hedge, and I also have about 25 sq.metres (30 sq.yds) of long grass –

it would be a gratuitous lie to describe it as a wildflower meadow. Both are cut once a year, and each generates a mountain of material that completely overwhelms the smooth running of my normal compost system. I don't have a shredder, so my hedge trimmings are taken away and composted by my local waste-disposal company. The "hay" from the "meadow" goes onto its own, open heap, which I occasionally excavate to retrieve quite decent compost from the bottom.

My two-bin system, made from salvaged timber, won't win awards for looks, but does the job.

Feeling the heat

If you're lucky enough to have a spare binful of compost in the spring, there's nothing to stop you growing plants directly in the heap itself. Make a small hole in the top of the heap, fill it with soil, and plant into that. Keep it well watered and the compost will provide everything else. This works well for greedy plants that enjoy a rich soil with plenty of nutrients.

One thing to bear in mind is that you should always start with sturdy, well-grown plants. Seeds or small seedlings will simply make a meal for slugs, although you could use the compost as a "hot bed" for trays of older seedling plants or cuttings. Also this is an option only if your compost bin is located in a sunny spot.

Possible plants Chilli peppers, courgettes or marrows, cucumbers, nasturtiums, petunias, potatoes, pumpkins and squashes, trailing tomatoes.

Warm roots make happy plants, whether they are nasturtiums or seedlings and cuttings.

Wormeries

A traditional, hot compost heap is too hot for anything other than bacteria to live in the core. But in a cool compost heap (and most are cool), a lot of the work is done by worms. So naturally worms have been domesticated in a composting process that relies entirely on worms. The result is the wormery.

HOW THEY WORK

The worms are variously known as brandlings, red worms, or tiger worms. They live in decaying organic matter and are not the same as ordinary garden earthworms, which live in the soil and would not thrive in a wormery.

Companies that supply wormeries will also supply worms, but they can be obtained more cheaply from fishing-tackle suppliers. Better still, simply collect some from your compost heap, or from a neighbour if you don't have one. Failing that, put a bag of fresh green waste with a hole in the bottom on any patch of bare earth and it will rapidly be colonized by suitable worms.

A wormery consists in its simplest form of two compartments: an upper chamber where the worms work, and a lower collection

sump where liquid collects. Since kitchen waste is mostly water, wormeries produce a lot of liquid: it's essential that this is kept away from the worms (which hate being waterlogged) and that it can easily be removed. Therefore I recommend that you consider only a wormery with a tap at the base. More complicated models consist of stacking trays with holes in their bases: the worms work their way up through the trays, leaving the finished compost (basically, worm poo) in the lower trays.

A wormery should be started off with a layer of old potting compost, garden compost, sawdust, or damp, shredded newspaper. The worms dislike acidity, so you need to take care over what you

put in. You can add most types of kitchen waste, ideally little and often. A wormery should cope without being fed for up to four weeks, so normal family holidays are no problem.

What goes in Coffee grounds, cooked citrus peel, cooked garlic, cooked onions, cooked rice and pasta, finely crushed eggshells, fruit, stale bread, tea bags, raw or cooked vegetables, small amounts of shredded paper (not glossy), small quantities of soft garden waste.

What stays out Anything spicy, salty, or vinegary, bones, dairy products, fat, fish, meat, tough autumn leaves, woody garden waste.

There's no need to empty a simple wormery with a single working chamber until it's full, which will take 6–12 months. Most of the worms will be in the top 20cm (8in), so just remove this layer, empty the bin, and then put the top layer back in and start again. Stacking-tray versions are simpler – just remove the lowest tray, empty it, and replace on the top.

Worm compost may be used in the same way as ordinary garden compost or as a constituent of home-made potting compost. The liquid makes an excellent plant food, after being diluted with ten parts of water to one of liquid feed.

FOR PET-LOVERS ONLY

Wormeries are not quite as simple as enthusiasts sometimes claim. Even when working perfectly, they can smell and they tend to attract flies, so I don't recommend keeping one in the kitchen. They don't like temperatures over 30°C (86°F), so in the summer they need to be somewhere shady outdoors. Equally, the worms will be killed if the wormery freezes solid, so they need to be somewhere frost-free during the winter. In fact, although worms don't hibernate, they work very slowly below about 10°C (50°F), so unless you can keep your wormery somewhere relatively warm in the winter, you will have to find something else to do with your kitchen waste during this period.

Coupled with an inability to deal with most kinds of garden waste, this means that you will really need a compost heap as well as a wormery, unless you don't have a garden at all.

Thousands of enthusiastic gardeners keep wormeries and will tell you how wonderful they are. However, I suggest that they are best considered as an intriguing and slightly challenging hobby, rather than as a reliable alternative to ordinary garden compost-making.

If you wouldn't even consider keeping rabbits or a hamster, then a wormery is probably not for you.

Using compost:
digging is for dummies

When is compost ready?

Or, to put it another way, how long is a piece
of string? All the dead plant material in
your garden would rot down and eventually
disappear of its own accord, without your
assistance, if you just left it alone. The same
would happen to green kitchen waste if you
just threw it out of the back door onto the
nearest flower bed. In practice, this means
that compost is ready when you think it is.

The high-fibre heap, based on paper, card, and soft, green
waste only, will produce a fine compost relatively quickly, in
which none of the original ingredients will be recognizable.
A heap that started out with a lot of woody material will look
twiggy for a lot longer.

From a garden-worthy perspective, the difference is
immaterial: both textures of compost will do exactly the same job
in the garden, equally effectively. The only reason to prefer fine
material – apart from its appearance – is if you plan to make your
own potting compost, for which coarse material is unsuitable.

Don't be misled into unrealistic expectations of your compost
heap. The compost shown tumbling invitingly out of the bins in

Judging when your compost
is finished is partly
a question of aesthetics.

gardening programmes and magazines has been carefully sieved to remove all the annoying, twiggy bits. Either that, or it came out of a sack of commercially produced soil conditioner.

In trials run in the UK by the Royal Horticultural Society, a mixture of green and shredded, woody garden waste was composted for 12 months. About 80 per cent of the resulting compost could be described as "fine" particles, that is, it would pass through a 10mm (½in) sieve. That's good enough for me, and

unless you want your flower beds to look like a Chelsea Flower Show garden, it should be good enough for you too.

Incidentally, the lack of any agreed method of deciding when it is finished is a major obstacle to the scientific investigation of compost. Science can study only things that can be measured fairly objectively.

Most plants love garden compost whatever its texture, but you might have to sieve compost for use in potting mixtures.

Where to use compost

For many gardeners, making and using compost still has a slightly old-fashioned air, a whiff of "dig-for-victory". It's therefore easy to get the impression that compost is only for the vegetable plot. There is some truth in this: the vegetable plot is the only part of the garden where all plant material is routinely harvested, and if you're taking a lot out, it pays to put something back in.

It's also in the vegetable plot that the effect of compost is most easily measured: tests show that you can expect application of a 5–10cm (2–4in) layer of garden compost to double yields of cabbages, leeks, or potatoes. Most other kinds of organic material will work just as well, but no better –

ordinary garden compost really is the **perfect balanced diet** for plants.

But compost will have exactly the same beneficial impact elsewhere in the garden, even if the effect can't be measured in kilograms or pounds. Your trees, shrubs, and herbaceous plants will grow bigger and have more flowers and fruit. What's more, there will be other benefits – your plants will be healthier and less affected by stresses such as drought and insect pests. In short,

you cannot have too much compost, anywhere in the garden.

Your soil will benefit from compost applied at any time of year, but to get the best results, spread garden compost (or any other organic material) while the soil is moist, to retain the moisture. In practice, this usually means any time from autumn through to spring. Winter rains may wash some nutrients out of compost applied in autumn, but on the plus side, the compost will help to protect the soil structure. Also, the worms will be able to work on it during any mild periods. Applying a layer at least 5cm (2in) thick will help to suppress weeds, and in any case you won't see much benefit if you spread compost around very thinly.

Even though everywhere in the garden will benefit from a mulch of compost or other organic matter, it's worth mentioning that mulching dramatically improves the establishment of newly planted trees and shrubs.

Having a dig?

Instructions for making compost often conclude by advising that it should be dug into the soil. But why? The world got on well enough for millions of years before the invention of the spade and garden fork, so digging can hardly be crucial to soil health.

The usual reason for digging in compost is to get it down to "where the plants need it". But earthworms are dedicated to doing just that, and the careful gardener takes a lot of trouble to encourage a healthy earthworm population. Moreover, earthworm activity is one of the major creators of good soil structure, while digging is one of the principal destroyers of that structure.

The fine fungal, or mycorrhizal, network that breaks down organic matter in the soil and transfers the resulting nutrients to plant roots is extensive, but delicate. It is also not improved by being chopped into small pieces during digging. In truth, there are only two good reasons for digging.

The first is to alleviate the effects of soil compaction, caused by trampling or machinery. The second is to remove deep-rooted perennial weeds such as docks, dandelions, and thistles.

Both these problems (if present) may need some digging initially, but once they are sorted out, further digging is unnecessary except as a source of exercise and fresh air. In any case, there's no need to take my word for it. Tests always show that compost applied as a mulch works just as well – in fact, sometimes better – as when it is dug in.

If organic matter with a high C:N ratio, such as straw or shredded prunings, is dug into the soil, it may promote the growth of soil microbes that will compete with plants for the soil's nitrogen. This is never a problem if the compost is incorporated slowly by earthworm activity, as happens with mulching, rather than by digging in.

MULCH, MARVELLOUS MULCH

When used as a mulch, garden compost will not
only improve the soil structure, but will also add
significant quantities of plant nutrients. The
nourishing effect will be most noticeable on light,
sandy soils, which tend to be deficient in nutrients,
while improvements in structure will be more
evident on heavy, clay soils.

There are other forms of bulky organic matter you could
use, as well as garden compost. If you're aiming to add nutrients
(for example in the vegetable plot), garden compost or a mulch of
lawn mowings are your best bet.

Leafmould or shredded prunings
add organic matter
but don't contain
many nutrients.

Among materials you might "import" to your
garden, straw, wood chips, and bark are also
low in nutrients, while cocoa shells and stable
manure are high in nutrients. Proprietary soil
conditioners are very variable – always read the
label for application rates.

Most forms of bulky organic matter, when applied to the soil, don't seem to have a very significant effect on the soil pH (acidity or alkalinity). In fact, results from mulching trials are somewhat contradictory, with the same type of mulch sometimes having opposite effects in different trials. The exception is mushroom compost, which is distinctly alkaline and therefore always has the effect of raising soil pH.

One reason for variations in the trials is that soils vary in pH to start with (*see page 33*). Another is that some soils, like clays, are much more resistant to changes in pH than others, such as sandy soils. The best advice for those who want to grow acid-loving plants such as camellias or rhododendrons is to be cautious and bear in mind the following:

- if your soil is naturally acid (with a low pH), your own garden compost is probably OK
- don't use any proprietary soil improver without first checking its pH – most are alkaline (with a high pH)
- avoid lavish use of highly alkaline mushroom compost – it can even damage plants that prefer a neutral soil
- to maintain soil acidity, chipped conifer bark or conifer leafmould are a good bet
- if you don't mind using garden chemicals, sulphur or ammonium sulphate should also work well.

Potting compost

There was a time when potting compost was a problem for green, organic gardeners. All the major brands were peat-based and if you wanted a peat-free, soil-less potting compost (that is, not a loam-based type), you had to make your own. Many of the early peat-free composts, based on coir or composted wood waste, performed poorly or were very variable.

Thankfully, things have changed and the best modern, peat-free composts are both reliable and perform extremely well. Nor will making your own compost from home-made ingredients give better results than the best commercial, peat-free brands. It will save you money but, unless you use a lot of potting compost, not a great deal. Having said all that, if you still want to make your own potting compost,

the key ingredient is
leafmould.

Why leafmould? Because ordinary garden compost is as variable, in pH and nutrient content, as the ingredients that were used to make it. It also often contains weed seeds. Leafmould is

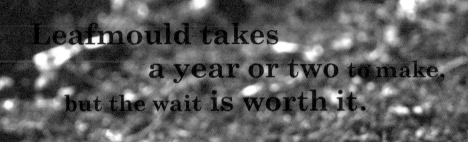

Leafmould takes a year or two to make, but the wait is worth it.

much more predictable and, crucially, can be relied on to be low in nutrients. It also has a nice open, but water-retentive, texture, and shouldn't contain weed seeds. In fact, pure leafmould makes an excellent seed compost.

Leafmould won't support seedling growth for more than a few days, so nutrients must be added for a compost with more staying power. One way of doing this is simply to add an organic fertilizer, for example blood, fish and bone, bonemeal, or hoof and horn, to leafmould. Seaweed meal is a useful substitute for those who don't like to use animal products.

If you are determined to stick to home-made ingredients, you can include sieved garden compost, which is very variable but generally quite nutrient-rich. Equal parts leafmould and garden compost is one possibility. Even neat garden compost should be alright for plants that need a lot of nutrients, like tomatoes. If you have a wormery, you could substitute worm compost for garden compost. Worm compost has the advantage of being weed-free, finely textured, and reliably rich in nutrients. Compost from a high-fibre heap shares these characteristics: it's worth having such a heap if you want to make a lot of potting compost.

Adding horticultural grit to any mix will add more "body" and improve the drainage. You can use garden loam, but many experts recommend that it's pasteurized first, and I think pasteurizing your own loam is beyond the average gardener.

If you decide to make your own potting compost, my advice is:

- treat it as a bit of an adventure, rather than as a cheap way of producing a reliable product – don't expect the "same" mixture always to give the same results
- make small quantities and don't try to store it
- water very carefully – your own mix will have quite different physical properties to any bought compost
- be alert to the plant's growth and feed it if necessary
- always check a mixture's pH before trying to grow acid-loving plants in it

No heap? No problem:
grow your own compost

Spreading it around

I've tended to assume that every sensible
gardener should have a compost heap, but
that's not strictly true. You may object to
the space needed by compost bins. Equally,
you may regard moving large quantities of
organic matter from all over the garden to
the compost heap – only to move it all back
again at a later date – as a pointless activity.
If so, fear not: even for the green gardener,
a compost heap is far from essential.

So if you don't have a compost heap, what do you do with all
your organic waste? Grass clippings may simply be left where they
are, on the lawn. They will look untidy for a short time, but they
will soon decompose and return their nutrients straight back to
where they came from. If you prefer to collect grass
clippings, they make an excellent, high-
nutrient mulch for any part of the
garden, especially the vegetable plot.

From lawn to veg plot: empty grass clippings
directly onto the soil to mulch your plants.

If you invest in a mulching lawn mower, or recycler mower, the grass clippings are finely chopped and forced into the turf, so you don't even see them. This is an attractive option if you have a large lawn and find it hard to know what to do with all the grass clippings, or if you spend a lot of money on lawn fertilizer. A recycler mower solves both problems.

A large herbaceous border may produce a good deal of green waste when it is tidied up at the end of the season, but there's a simple solution here.

Just cut everything down and
leave it where it falls.

This will look untidy during the winter, but it's good for wildlife, which will shelter under it, and will soon be covered up by the fresh growth in the spring.

Autumn leaves and shredded woody material also make excellent mulches, and don't really need to be processed through a compost heap. You may be told that these low-nutrient materials will "rob" your soil of nitrogen, and so they will – but only if you dig them in. Apply them as a mulch and this problem disappears.

You may also read that freshly shredded, woody prunings will release toxic chemicals that will harm your plants, but there is little or no evidence for this. The main problem is that freshly

Spring growth soon covers up the evidence of old shoots cut down after last year.

shredded material doesn't look very nice, but it soon ages and blends in. If this bothers you, just leave the fresh material in a heap to age for a month or so. Not much decomposition will happen during this time, but the material will look a lot better.

Downsizing your lawn or making a new vegetable plot? Skim off the old turf with a spade and stack it, grass-side down, for at least a year. It should rot down into a nice, crumbly loam which you can then use as a mulch or to top-dress the lawn.

That leaves kitchen waste. One option is a wormery (*see pages 140–145*) but, if you have a vegetable plot, there are others. A small compost bin could be incorporated into the crop-rotation cycle in a vegetable plot (*see page 133*), but if you want to do this, why bother with a bin at all?

The usual objections to open compost heaps are that they aren't very attractive and that many of the nutrients are leached away into the soil, but

neither of these is a serious problem if your heap occupies a spare bit of the vegetable plot.

If you think this makes your garden look too much like a third-world shanty-town, there are more organized variations on the same theme.

First, it helps to divide your plot into conveniently sized beds and edge them with boards, bricks, or stones. These will help to stop your compost migrating on to the paths. You can now buy recycled plastic boards that slot neatly together and do the same job with no effort at all.

Second, cover your chosen bed with a good layer of newspaper or cardboard and water it well. This continuous layer will prevent weeds from becoming a problem. Finally, add layers of kitchen waste and, ideally, grass clippings as they become available.

Once you have accumulated a layer about 15cm (6in) thick, just leave it for a few months (or over winter), watering during dry spells. You can then plant your vegetables directly through the now-decomposed, organic layer. No need to dig.

Meanwhile, start the whole process again on another bed in the plot.

Food for soil

You can't have too much compost. A useful
extra source of organic matter, principally
for the vegetable garden or any temporarily
unoccupied bit of the garden, is a green
manure. This is any crop deliberately grown
for a few months and then killed to return
the organic matter to the soil.

The benefits of green manures
- primarily, adding extra organic matter
- they protect the soil structure from damage by heavy rain,
  especially if present over the winter
- they retain nutrients that might otherwise be washed out of
  the soil – some deep-rooted green manures, such as alfalfa,
  can bring extra nutrients from deeper layers of soil
- their roots can help to break up heavy soils
- they suppress weeds
- crops from the bean family capture nitrogen from the air
- they could be used as part of a pest-control strategy –
  sowing a low-growing green manure such as clover beneath
  brassicas is reputed to reduce damage by cabbage root fly

Clover fixes nitrogen from
the air and suppresses weeds
until the sweet corn
has been harvested.

CHOOSING YOUR GREENS

Many gardening books will provide details of the different green manures that are available. There are several important things to bear in mind when choosing one.

Nutrients If you want to add (rather than merely conserve) nutrients, you need a leguminous manure, that is, one from the bean family. These include alfalfa (also called lucerne), clover (alsike, crimson, or red), fenugreek, field beans, lupin, medick, or winter tares.

Hardiness Most green manures are hardy and can withstand frost, but some, such as clover, field beans, grazing rye, and winter tares, are particularly suitable for growing over winter. On the other hand, you might find a less hardy green manure is not so much trouble: buckwheat, fenugreek, or phacelia will be killed off by the first hard frost.

Growth rate If you want a green manure to fill in a short gap in a border or vegetable patch in summer, you need something fast-growing. Mustard is ideal.

Green manures: (*from top left, clockwise*) mustard, clover, phacelia, and alfalfa.

Crop rotation Many green manures are closely related to vegetable crops, and you need to consider this when sowing. Leguminous green manures shouldn't directly follow peas or beans, and mustard is prone to all the same pests and diseases as brassicas like cabbages and pak choi.

Fringe benefits It's not recommended to let green manures set seed; and if they do, some of them can become troublesome weeds. However, if you do let them flower, some green manures will attract pollinating insects. Most insects like buckwheat, and phacelia is loved by bees.

Cost Green-manure seeds are broadcast sown, rather than sown in rows. It also helps to sow at high density to smother weeds. This means you could use a lot of seeds, so cost is an important consideration.

Many green manures are agricultural crops, so it pays to check agricultural seed merchants, where you will find the seeds being sold much more cheaply than from garden shops or websites. Always check, however, whether agricultural seeds have been treated with fungicides or other chemicals.

Use your initiative!

Books and magazines somehow manage to imply that there is something special about the plants normally listed as green manures. There isn't. You can grow almost anything that takes your fancy as a green manure. If you feed the birds you may have a big sack of sunflower seeds, so why not try those? The cheapest green manure is a good crop of annual weeds (but this is not recommended!).

Sunflowers for green manures must be cut when young: tough, old stems won't rot easily.

CUTTING THE MUSTARD

Guidance on growing green manures usually ends with the advice that they should be dug into the soil, but there's really no need to do this. Green manures are often sown in late summer or autumn, when annual flower beds and vegetable plots are being cleared. The simplest option is to grow a manure that isn't cold-hardy and let the frost kill the plants for you.

More often, however, you want a green manure to protect the soil over the winter, then to get rid of it before sowing or planting new crops in the spring. Here,

the simplest solution is to cut down the green manure in the spring with a grass strimmer.

You could also chop it with a spade, if it has a nice, sharp edge. Then cover it with old carpet, black plastic, or newspaper until the manure has rotted. The beauty of newspaper is that it will rot along with the manure so you need do nothing else.

Alternatively, if you have a binful of compost, use that to cover the manure. Whatever you do, leave at least a month before sowing or planting new crops.

If, despite my advice, you decide to dig in your green manure, you might want to consider growing one that's relatively easy to dig. Alfalfa and grazing rye are hard work, while buckwheat, fenugreek, mustard (*see opposite*), and phacelia are easy. Any green manure will be easier to dig in (and will rot more quickly) while it is still young.

Troubleshooting

Nothing doing in your heap?

It's probably too dry or too low in nitrogen. These problems often go together, since coarse, woody material has a very open structure that retains little moisture and easily dries out.

The simple solution is to try watering the heap and see if that makes any difference. A better idea is to tackle the basic problem and add more nitrogen-rich material, such as grass clippings or kitchen waste. Or you could try watering with dilute urine.

Low temperatures could also be to blame. If a heap constructed in autumn does nothing during the winter, wait to see if summer solves the problem before taking any action. If the heap is dry and undecomposed around the edges, your bin probably has too much ventilation. If it's dry on top, it needs a lid.

Rancid or sulphurous smells

mean there's a shortage of oxygen somewhere in your heap – the exact opposite of the previous problem. It is caused by water-logging or poor structure, that is, too much green waste – especially grass – at one go.

If your bin doesn't have a waterproof lid, then maybe it should. If you suspect the mixture is at fault, add more dry, carbon-rich materials. Dry cardboard is the ideal material for an emergency mopping-up operation.

Rarely, a compost heap may smell of ammonia. This is a sure sign of excess nitrogen, and may mean there is too much nitrogen-rich material, or it may be caused by over-zealous use of compost activators. Add more paper, leaves, or other carbon-rich material, and use compost activators only if you are sure your heap is short of nitrogen.

If the heap collapses in a wet, slimy mess,

the problem is too much soft, green material, especially grass clippings. See above.

Weed seeds are killed

only by a really hot heap, and even then the kill will not be complete. The best solution is not to add weed seeds to the heap in the first place; try to clear annual weeds before they seed. An uncovered heap may acquire weed seeds, so use a covered bin.

Flies around the heap: larvae of

many flies feed on decaying organic matter, so flies are a normal part of the composting process. The flies you are most likely to notice are fruit flies. As their name suggests, they are attracted by fruit, so make sure that fruit waste is buried beneath other compost material such as grass clippings.

Adult flies tend to build up in bins from

which they cannot escape, so are less of a problem in a bin that isn't completely sealed.

- ## Pests or processors?
  A successful compost heap will contain many woodlice, slugs, millipedes, centipedes, and other invertebrates. These are not a problem!

- ## Rats: compost heaps often get blamed for attracting rats, but are rarely the main cause of the problem. Cooked food, meat, or fish will attract rats, so do not put these on your compost heap unless you are using a rodent-proof bin. Since few compost bins are rodent-proof, this amounts to a complete ban on such waste for the average gardener. Rodent-proof food composters do exist, but are outside the scope of this book.

Rats may visit compost heaps if they are already in the area, but other factors are much more important in increasing the probability of rats in the neighbourhood. These include garden livestock (rabbits, chickens, caged birds), overgrown and generally very untidy gardens, proximity to agricultural activities, and buildings in a poor state of repair.

Mice occasionally nest in my compost heap, but is that a problem? I don't think so.

Finally, relax.

Making compost is not like wallpapering the front room
or fixing a leaking tap, which can be done so badly that
you wish you'd never started. When it comes to making
compost, time and the tendency of all systems towards
a state of disorder are on your side.

Even if you do *everything* wrong, you will still make decent compost eventually.

Useful addresses

Cornell University has a website section on composting, **http://compost.css.cornell. edu/Composting_Homepage. html**. It comes as close as anything on the net to telling you everything you need to know about composting. The web pages are particularly strong on the science of composting.

The Composting Association (**www.compost. org.uk**) exists mainly for the composting industry, but the website has a section on home composting for gardeners.

Cool Composting: a fresh approach. This factsheet from the Centre for Alternative Technology (CAT), in Wales in the UK, describes the high-fibre composting system developed there. Order from the CAT website: **www.cat.org.uk**

www.digitalseed.com is a good site from southern California, with an emphasis on composting in dry climates.

Garden Organic, formerly the Henry Doubleday Research Association (HDRA), have lots of good practical advice on composting. See **www. gardenorganic.org.uk**

Gardening Which? (**www. which.net/gardeningwhich**) magazine tests composting products, including bins, and is completely independent, so does not take advertising. There is no comparable gardening magazine anywhere else in the world.

www.greencone.com sell two devices that are claimed to compost everything, including raw and cooked meat or fish, bones, and dairy products.

www.greenventure.ca has good links to several composting sites, including several with advice on composting pet waste.

The Humanure Handbook by Joseph Jenkins is free online at **www.weblife.org/humanure,** and is worth a try for those who want to go even farther and compost human waste.

www.livingsoil.co.uk advises on the Bokashi system of waste digestion. It will compost all kitchen waste, including meat and fish scraps.

Organic Gardening magazines are published in the UK and USA. They both often have articles on composting. See **www. organicgardeningmagazine. co.uk** and **www.organicgardening.com**

The Royal Horticultural Society (**www.rhs.org.uk**) provides advice on all aspects of gardening, including composting and wormeries. *The Garden*, the RHS magazine, sometimes has articles on composting, and the annual report of the RHS Science Departments includes information about their latest research on composting.

www.troubleatmill.com/ wormbin.htm provides instructions for making your own, cheap wormery.

The UK Waste and Resources Action Programme (**www.wrap. org.uk**) is a government-sponsored initiative with lots of advice on recycling and has a home-composting website: **www.recyclenow.com/home_ composting**

Index

Acknowledgements

Author's acknowledgements
Thanks to everyone at Dorling Kindersley, including Clare Shedden and Helen Fewster, as well as Peter Anderson, Alison Donovan, Jo Doran, Peter Luff, Rachael Smith, and Louise Waller. Thanks also to Anna Kruger for asking me to write the book in the first place, but a very special thank you to my editor, Annelise Evans, for her enthusiasm, knowledge, and ability to know what I wanted to say even before I knew myself.

Richard Gianfrancesco at *Gardening Which?* and Paul Alexander, at the Royal Horticultural Society, were both willing to answer my daft questions.

Finally thanks to my wife, Pat, for her uncompromising refusal to accept my second-best efforts, and to Pat, Lewis, and Rowan for their willingness to tolerate the author at work.

Publisher's acknowledgements
Dorling Kindersley would like to thank Gerry and Sylvia Smith and Bill Watkin for generously allowing us to photograph their compost bins, and Sharon and Ivan Gould for letting us photograph in their home. Thanks also to Clare Sheddon and Peter Anderson for modelling, and to Sandy Lelliott for help with photoshoot preparation.

Photographic credits
Dorling Kindersley would like to thank the following for their kind permission to reproduce their photographs: p.15: Louie Psihoyos/CORBIS; p.21, centre pp.32–33, and p.166: Steven Wooster; p.67: Lotti de la Bedoyere; p.137: Ken Thompson.

All new photography by Peter Anderson.

All other images © DK Images.
For further information, see:
www.dkimages.com